Stop Playing Church

Chris,
I am grateful that we get
to do Life together
Blessings

Stop Playing Church

A Call for Authentic Discipleship

Doug Franklin

XULON PRESS ELITE

Xulon Press Elite
2301 Lucien Way #415
Maitland, FL 32751
407.339.4217
www.xulonpress.com

Unless otherwise indicated, Scripture quotations taken from the Holy Bible, New International Version (NIV). Copyright © 1973, 1978, 1984, 2011 by Biblica, Inc.™. Used by permission. All rights reserved.

Scripture quotations taken from The Message (MSG). Copyright © 1993, 1994, 1995, 1996, 2000, 2001, 2002. Used by permission of NavPress Publishing Group. Used by permission. All rights reserved.

Paperback ISBN-13: 978-1-6628-3891-0
Ebook ISBN-13: 978-1-6628-3892-7

To my wife and children – Nicole, Tucker, Tanner, Delaney & Darbey. Thank you for your sacrifices and support so that I can be real about who I am and whose I am. GO TEAM FRANKLIN!

Table of Contents

Introduction

"Stop!"

It has been referred to as "The first law of holes." An adage whose original source is unclear and goes like this, "If you find yourself in a hole, stop digging." The adage refers to those times and situations where we've found ourselves going in the wrong direction or in the midst of difficult circumstances. The first thing we need to do is stop doing what we are doing, the action that created the current conditions. You can't get out of a hole by continuing to dig. You can't get out of debt by continuing to spend money that you don't have. You can't break bad habits by continuing to do them. The first thing we must do is *stop*.

A few years ago, I was invited to preach at a church revival. Whenever I am invited to come into someone else's church to preach, I will always ask them if there might be something that they would like me to preach about. Maybe there is a theme of the revival, or they might be focusing on a certain topic. On this occasion, the pastor told me he "...Wanted to hear a word from God's prophet. Whatever God is laying on your heart to share with His church."

As I thought about the directions from my friend and then prayed, I felt in the depth of my soul that there was a word that God had for me to share. While I certainly don't claim to be a prophet and it is extremely humbling each time someone tells me that they have felt God speaking to them through my preaching, I did feel that I have word to share. The word that cried out in my Spirit as I thought about what to say to the Church was *stop!* Stop playing church! Stop! Stop pretending! Stop hiding! Stop trying to be something that we are not! Just stop! Stop playing church!

In this moment of prayer, I was overcome with the sense of urgency and importance that all of us who claim to follow Jesus need to get real about who we are and who God is. We need to be real about our love for God and our love for one another. There is too much at stake for us to *play church.* We will never experience the life that God has for us – the one that we long for – if we keep playing church. *The first thing we must do is stop.* It is time for us to refuse to play church anymore. We can't continue to play church and expect a different outcome. We can't keep hiding behind stained glass facades, "churchy" behaviors, or the next great church program. We must live the new way of life that Jesus invites us to live. We must stop playing church and start following Jesus with our lives.

We all long for God to be real. We want our faith to be real. We all desire to experience the power and presence of Christ in our lives. *Stop Playing Church* is my cry for authentic discipleship. A cry to stop pretending, stop acting how "Christians act" and doing things "Christians do." We should be followers of Jesus.

I have written this for anyone who believes there must be something more to life. It is for anyone who has been turned off or turned away by organized religion. This book is for Christians who are tired of feeling like they are just going through the motions.

Stop Playing Church is for church leaders who desire to lead people to deeper love and commitment to Christ. This is a book about real spiritual disciplines and discipleship. Authentic discipleship is being fully committed Christ and transparent about who we are, who God is, and genuine about living in relationship with the Christ. It is about being authentic as we live as the church. My cry is to take discipleship seriously as well as the command to love God and to love our neighbors. I will present a discipleship that is grounded in a biblical understanding of what it means to follow Christ every moment of every day.

Stop Playing Church intentionally erases the line between the sacred and the secular so that all of life is lived in the power, presence, and grace of God. This book is a challenge to reimagine church as a way of living and not just something that we do or somewhere we go once or twice a week. It is a challenge to get real about life, about love, and about our relationship with Christ. It is a challenge to step out of hiding, to take off your mask, and to be who you are without shame because you are a child of God.

I will share from my own personal experiences as one who has struggled with playing church and living authentic faith as well as my twenty-plus years of experience as a pastor and church leader to illustrate what is meant by *playing church* and *authentic discipleship*. I will draw on biblical truths to teach about the cost of playing church and the implications on our lives. My approach will take a biblical perspective of spiritual disciplines in everyday life and an understanding church as a way of life. This book invites us to embrace the freedom of vulnerability as we live our lives empowered by the Holy Spirit connecting to God and others as we do life together.

It invites us to stop playing church.

Part I:
A Call for Authentic Discipleship

Chapter 1:
Playing Church

"Adam and his wife were both naked, and they felt no shame" (Gen. 2:25).

Then the eyes of both of them were opened, and they realized they were naked; so they sewed fig leaves together and made coverings for themselves. Then the man and his wife heard the sound of the Lord God as he was walking in the garden in the cool of the day, and they hid from the Lord God among the trees of the garden. But the Lord God called to the man, "Where are you?" He answered, "I heard you in the garden, and I was afraid because I was naked; so I hid." Genesis 3:7-10

P laying church is not a new thing. It is not something that has come about in the past few years, or even decades or centuries, and I am certainly not the first person to write or speak about it. In fact, throughout this book, we are going to be looking at some teaching from Jesus and many scriptures in the Bible that speak on the matter. However, I do think that it is helpful at the onset to define what is meant by *playing church.* Certainly, if we are going to stop doing something, we must first know what it is.

In a broad sense, what I am referring to when I am saying *playing church,* I am talking about actions, behaviors, or appearances that we substitute for a relationship with Jesus. Playing church is focused on doing and not on being. Playing church mistakes religious activity for a relationship with Jesus. It is pretending that we are something we are not. It is hiding who we are from one another. It is trying to look like we have it all together on the outside while we are falling apart on the inside. It is talking about Jesus but not walking with Him. It is confining a relationship with Jesus to certain times, locations, and actions. Playing church compartmentalizes the sacred and the secular. It has a spiritual life, a work-life, and a home life rather than a Jesus life. Playing church is doing anything other than being in relationship with Jesus. It is allowing our actions and behaviors to replace the relationships we are created to live in. We are created to be in relationship with God and one another. When we substitute actions and behaviors for these relationships, we are playing church.

When we look at the creation story in Genesis chapter 2, we get a picture of the relationship that God desires for us to have with Him and one another. Before Adam and Eve ate of the forbidden fruit, we get a glimpse of God's intent and what a real relationship with God and one another looks like. God is with them in the garden. There is no separation between God and the creation. They are *doing life* together.

God has said it is not good to be alone. God has provided a suitable helper for Adam, and they are all living in relationship with each other. We are told in the last verse of chapter 2 that "Adam and his wife were both naked, and they felt no shame." Why are we told they are naked? I think that it is because we need to understand just how close this relationship is and how powerful. Naked is not just that they have no clothes on, it is that they could be who they are. No hiding. No pretending. Being completely exposed to the other. The verse goes on to say, "and they felt no shame." They were not ashamed of who they were. They could be real. They could be honest. Without shame.

The interesting thing that happens is that as soon as they do what God asked them not to do, they went into hiding. They began by covering themselves up because they don't want to be seen for who they are. They hide in the garden and hope that God doesn't see them and know what they did. They seem to think that if they can make a change in their outward appearance, they might be able to hide what is going on. If they hide well enough then maybe what is really going on will go unnoticed. It is safe to say that Adam and Eve were the first to play church. They believed the serpent's lies and substituted their actions and behaviors for a relationship with God. They covered themselves and hide from God In order to pretend they were something that they were not. They were the first to think that if they just changed what was seen, maybe no one will notice who they really are.

Here are some thoughts that are both powerful and amazing. God didn't stop loving them when He found them hiding. God didn't stop desiring a real and authentic relationship with them after they ate from the tree that He'd strictly forbidden. Certainly, the consequences of their behavior altered things. No longer could they eat from the tree of life. No longer could they live in the garden. From now on they would toil, there would be pain in childbirth. Relationships have been impacted but they are not eliminated. In fact, God's love and desire for a relationship with us, His creation, doesn't change one bit. God understands our guilt and shame, and He provides clothing for us to cover our shame.

God loves us and desires a relationship with us so much that He provides for us when we can't do for ourselves. We all struggle with good and evil. He takes care of what is necessary to restore us back into a right relationship with Him. This is the good news that Jesus, through His death and resurrection, restores us back into a right relationship with God. We can have and enjoy life with God. We have new life in Christ. We are saved by grace, through faith. God desires a relationship with us and there is nothing that we can do, will do, or have done that will change this. But don't miss this, God does not want religious actions, good behavior, or proper theology if they are a substitute for the relationship that you were created for and Jesus died for you to have.

God did not create you to be a church-goer. He created you to live in *relationship* with Him. Don't substitute church attendance for a relationship with Jesus. Spiritual disciplines will help us to connect to God and grow in relationship with Jesus, but we cannot substitute them for doing life with God and others. We can't hide behind actions, behaviors, or outward appearances. We need to get real about who we are and whose we are. We need to get real about loving God and loving others. We need to get real about living in relationship with Jesus.

Jesus warns the church of His day about this type of behavior and points to how easy is for us to replace our relationship with religion. He gives a few illustrations of what playing church looked like in his day.

> *Everything they do is done for people to see: They make their phylacteries wide and the tassels on their garments long; they love the place of honor at banquets and the most important seats in the synagogues; they love to be greeted with respect in the marketplaces and to be called 'Rabbi' by others.* Matthew 23:5-7

> *Woe to you, teachers of the law and Pharisees, you hypocrites! You clean the outside of the cup and dish, but inside they are full of greed and self-indulgence. Blind Pharisee! First clean the inside of the cup and dish, and then the outside also will be clean. Woe to you, teachers of the law and Pharisees, you hypocrites! You are like whitewashed tombs, which look beautiful on the outside but on the inside are full of the bones of the dead and everything unclean. In the same way, on the outside you appear to people as righteous but, on the inside, you are full of hypocrisy and wickedness.* Matthew 23:25-28

Playing church doesn't look the same for everyone. We are clever and creative people. For us to truly define what we are doing in playing church requires open honesty on our part. It takes us looking at ourselves and examining our motives, our intentions, and our actions. It can't be defined as just one thing, one behavior or action. Playing church can be obvious behavior and it can be subtle. It happens when we lose sight of living in relationship with Jesus. When we replace that relationship with something else.

I should probably say something at this time about spiritual disciplines, rituals, church attendance, Bible studies, and other actions and practices that we participate in. These activities can sometimes become a replacement for living in relationship with Jesus. I am not saying that we must stop doing these things. I am not saying that we stop doing anything that helps us connect to God and to others and live out our relationship with Jesus.

We will take up the spiritual disciplines and being the church in the second part of the book. I am convinced that we need each other to do life with Jesus. We need to *be the church* to help one another connect and grow in relationship with Christ. We live out our love for God through our love for our neighbors.

I am going to suggest a way of understanding church and spiritual disciplines that keeps our relationship with God at the center of everything that we do. It takes a view of spiritual disciplines combined with being the church that refuses to play church. It takes a church body who refuses to let anything substitute or replace a relationship with Jesus and nurtures people in being real about who they are, about their love for God, and living in relationship with God and one another.

Can you imagine, being exactly who you are, no hiding, no pretending, being you in all your glory and feeling no shame? Can you imagine living openly and not hiding your hurts, weaknesses, struggles, or difficulties? Can you imagine knowing that you are not alone and that God's grace is enough for you? Can you imagine if there was a community of people who lived real lives, not hiding the truth from one another?

Here is some important truths – God loves you the way you are, no matter what you've done? With Jesus, you need not be ashamed. Christ offers forgiveness for our sins and covers us with His righteousness all we have to do is turn to him. You don't have to pretend that your Christian life is perfect and free from anger and that your family life is constant bliss. The Holy Spirit can empower us to form authentic communities of people who are real about who they are and real about living in relationship with God. Communities that claim they don't have all the answers or have it all figured out, but are being real about living in relationship with God and each other. Real about loving God and loving their neighbor. Real about doing life with Jesus and each other. Real about not playing church but being the church.

The reality is that God is walking with us and he is calling us to come out of hiding. He is inviting us to do life with Him. To walk with Him through our homes, workplaces, communities, churches, and all the other *gardens* we find ourselves in. Doing life means to live each moment, the good, bad, and ugly, with

Him. He is inviting us to a 24/7 relationship. Walking with Him through all our ordinary, everyday moments. He is inviting us to know that He loves us just the way we are and that he loves us enough to never abandon us to do life alone. He loves enough to clothe us in his grace, love, and righteousness as we walk with Him through our lives. And God invites us to do this together in relationship with one another – connecting to Him and others. To care for, nurture, and support each other in growing in relationship with Jesus. To laugh together, rejoice, cry, mourn and celebrate all of life together.

But we can't do this and still play church.

For us to fully experience this relationship we must stop hiding. We must stop hiding behind religious acts and "churchy" talk. We must stop pretending that we have it all figured out. We have to stop hiding behind our Sunday-best masks and our religious "to do and don't do lists." We must stop playing church.

Chapter 2:
The Cost of Playing Church

Then Jesus said to the crowds and to his disciples: "The teachers of the law and the

Pharisees sit in Moses' seat. So you must be careful to do everything they tell you.

But do not do what they do, for they do not practice what they preach. Matthew 23:1-3

One day as Jesus was teaching the crowds and his disciples, He used the church people of the day, the teachers of the law, and the Pharisees as an example to talk about what authentic discipleship should be like. However, His approach was not to point at these "good church folks" and say, "That is what it looks like." Instead, He says, "Do not do what they do." Jesus, as he begins to teach about real discipleship, tells his disciples, the crowds, and us that we have to be careful do the things that the teachers of the law are teaching *but* **don't** do what they are doing.

Throughout the rest of Matthew chapter 23, Jesus points out how we can play church and the dangers of playing church. Jesus wants us to understand that there is a great deal at stake when we are playing church. Jesus wants us to know that playing church comes at a cost. A cost that is too great, according to Jesus. There is just too much at stake to play church.

What's at Stake

I studied history during my undergraduate time. In war, and in many other things, when the cost becomes too great, people surrender. When the price is too much, people bow out, they stop. As long as the cost is not too much, battles will still be fought but when the amount of resources needed and the price paid is too much, that is when you find a surrender. The victor is proclaimed.

The other side of this is that the more people have at stake the greater the cost that they are willing to pay. Wars of Independence don't go by the same script as wars about occupation or territorial expansion. In wars of independence, people's independence is at stake. People are willing to pay a higher price when it comes to their freedom. Underdogs win in wars of independence. The little guy can defeat the giant when it comes to personal freedom. When our very lives are at stake we are willing to stake our lives on the outcome. When we have something meaningful and worthwhile for doing what we do, then we are "all in" because there is too much at stake.

So, what is at stake when we play church? What do we risk losing if our faith is not real or authentic? According to Jesus's teaching, we risk *everything*. I know that seems a little dramatic. But I think that this is exactly what Jesus is saying. Jesus points out the behavior of saying one thing and doing another and says, "Don't do that." Because there is too much at stake. We must stop playing church because our very lives and souls are at stake.

> Woe to you, teachers of the law and Pharisees, you hypocrites! You shut the door of the kingdom of heaven in people's faces. You yourselves do not enter, nor will you let those enter who are trying to.

> Woe to you, teachers of the law and Pharisees, you hypocrites! You travel over land and sea to win a single convert, and when you have succeeded, you make them twice as much a child of hell as you are. Matthew 23:13-15

For Jesus, our relationship with Him is at stake. When we play church, it impacts our relationship with God. Playing church also impacts other people's relationships with God. That is what is a stake. Our connection to God is at stake as well as the power of the Holy Spirit at work in our lives. Living life to the full. Forgiveness, new life, the power to overcome sin and death. A relationship with the God who created us and loves us is at stake when we play church. This is why we have to stop. Because playing church is closing the door to the kingdom of God. Stop playing church because it is keeping us from experiencing the love and grace of God in our lives. Stop playing church because it is leading to our deaths.

Playing church is killing us.

On top of what playing church is doing to us, it is also impacting the lives of others. When we play church, according to Jesus, two things can happen as we encounter others. Both of which lead to destruction for others. First, by playing church, our actions can keep people from entering the kingdom of God and close the door to a relationship with God for them. We have seen this happen. Too often, I have heard people say that they have been turned off to faith and to church because of what some church person has done to them or said to them. People have been hurt by people playing church and church people have done mean and hurtful things. People who don't know Jesus see this behavior and *say, I don't want anything to do with Jesus if that is the difference He makes in someone's life*. With false behavior, damaged emotions, and possible judgment, their door to God closes. People are turned off by the hypocrisy and they think Jesus must not be real because the people who say they are following him are fake. The door is closed.

The second thing that Jesus points out as a way our playing church impacts the lives of others is that we will lead them to do exactly what we are doing. By our behavior, we will convince others to play church with us. This too leads to destruction. It leads to separation from God, emptiness, and death. We see this as well. Most Sundays we can see some of the best acting there is on the planet. We have all been taught how to act in church. We watch each other and we think we see people who have it all together so we pretend to have it all together too, even though before we walked into the sanctuary we were falling apart.

By having been taught "how to act," we're sending a message that's a lie. The funny thing is that the person we think has it all together really doesn't. They are just acting. We are all just playing church. If we do draw people to that kind of church then they imitate our behavior, which is killing us, and it leads to their destruction as well.

Our acting troop grows but not the kingdom of God. We build churches but no one's life is changed by the power of God. We grasp treasures on earth, but the treasure of the kingdom of God remains out of reach. We must stop playing church because it is surely killing the church. It is leading people away from Jesus – not to Him. Playing church shuts the doors to the kingdom of God.

If we look at the state of the church in America, we can see this. Church attendance is not what it once was. Participation in the church continues to decline. If you speak to people who are not Christians, what you find is not that they have never heard about Jesus or experienced the church. In America, most people have been exposed to the church and many people have been turned off and even turned away. I hey have been hurt by the church. They see a disconnect between what church people say and what they do. They see nothing real about church. Talk to someone who has left the church and it won't take long before you hear the word that Jesus used in Matthew 23 to describe the Pharisees and the teachers of the law.

The witnesses that we are for Christ to the world is distorted and even at times completely false. Research has revealed that many people describe the church with the words hypocritical, judgmental, and insensitive.[1] Clearly, these are not words that we would use to describe Jesus.

The Bible teaches mercy, compassion, and grace. Jesus teaches us to practice what we preach[2] and to not just be hearers of the Word but doers of the Word[3]. Jesus teaches directly that we are not to judge[4]. Jesus tells us in Matthew 23 not to do what the Pharisees and the teachers of the law are doing and to practice what we preach. We are not to say one thing yet do another.

Playing church, as Jesus points out, drives people away from Jesus and leads to a crisis in the church. The very lives of people desiring to be saved are at stake. It can fool us into a false sense of hope. False hope is really no hope at all.

But we do have hope. Jesus comes to bring life not death. He comes to bring the kingdom of heaven to us. He opens the door. He makes a way. He invites us to make Him our lives. It is an invitation to be real about who we are and who we belong to. He offers an invitation to all, to stop pretending,

---

[1] Kinnaman, David, and Gabe Lyons. 2007 Unchristian: what a new generation really thinks about Christianity—and why it matters. Grand Rapids, Mich: Baker Books.

[2] Matthew 23:3

[3] James 1:22

[4] Matthew 7:1-3, Luke 36-38

stop hiding, and be real about our need for Jesus and our love of God and neighbor.

As we read in Matthew 23, we should allow the chapter to speak to us about the cost of professing one thing but doing another. We need to recognize what is at stake when we hide who we really are and pretend that we are something that we are not. We need to hear Jesus's words to not "do what they do." We need to live out our faith in real and tangible ways. It is time to stop playing church. There is too much at stake. Our very lives and the lives of those we love are at stake. The church is dying. We are dying.

Therefore, we must take the words of Jesus seriously. We need to be serious about what it means to be a follower of Jesus and what it means to be the body of Christ redeemed by His blood. We need to have a biblical, Christ-centered under-standing of church and discipleship. The cost is too great for us not to strive to have a faith that is real and a discipleship that is authentic. There is just too much at stake.

Chapter 3:
Playing Church is Too Easy...
But it is Hard

Woe to you, teachers of the law and Pharisees, you hypocrites! You clean the outside of the cup and dish, but inside they are full of greed and self-indulgence. Blind Pharisee! First clean the inside of the cup and dish, and then the outside also will be clean. "Woe to you, teachers of the law and Pharisees, you hypocrites! You are like whitewashed tombs, which look beautiful on the outside but on the inside are full of the bones of the dead and everything unclean. In the same way, on the outside you appear to people as righteous but on the inside you are full of hypocrisy and wickedness.

Matthew 23:25-28

I am not sure if the teachers of the law or the Pharisees would have said at that time that they were playing church. They probably thought that their faith was real and authentic. They, as Jesus pointed out, believe that they have it all figured out. They know the right things to say and what they should do. They played the part of religious people very well. I bet that they took offense at Jesus's teaching that calls them "hypocrites." The word *hypocrite* comes from the Greek word *hypokrites*, which means *an actor*. It is someone who plays a part, pretends to be something or someone that they are not.

I'm sure that the church people in Jesus's day thought they were doing the best they could to live out their relationship with God. Many people have been credited for saying "Religion is man's attempt to reach God and Christianity is God's attempt to reach man." The Pharisees and the teacher of the law, I want to believe, were sincere in trying to reach God and they were doing what their religion had taught them. They were trying to adhere to the law. They weren't insincere. They weren't looking to shut the door on the kingdom of God. They were seeking to know God. But they were so consumed by their attempts at a religious life that they were unable to see God when he was in their midst.

In essence, the Pharisees were so focused on their *religious* life – following the letter of the law – that they failed to see the invitation to a relationship with God. They were trying so hard to do God *stuff* that they were missing God right in front of them offering new life.

The Ease of Playing Church and Not Noticing

Sometimes I tell people that I was drafted into ministry from the unranked. I was someone who did not grow up in the church. I went to church enough as a child to get my feet wet. Literally and figuratively. I was baptized in a Catholic church

19

as an infant and later, as a child, I was baptized in a Baptist church. I went to Sunday school and church from time to time as a kid but was in no way regular in my attendance. I learned enough about God to have an idea of God and enough about the devil to be sacred of him. This was the basic depth of my understanding of God and religion.

After the age of twelve, I really stopped going to church altogether. Throughout junior high and high school, I really don't even remember discussions about God or about the church. I would probably say at this time I believed there was a God, but I didn't bother Him and He didn't bother me. All of this changed in my twenties and when I became a parent.

When my wife was pregnant with our first child, Tucker, there were several school shootings in the news. Sadly, this is far too common in our world. My wife Nicole and I discussed how we were going to bring a child into this world and how we could parent under such circumstances. Full disclosure—we were scared! I remember talking to her about how I was an ornery child but, somehow I knew it was not right to do the things that we were hearing on the news. I remember thinking that my understanding of right and wrong must have been influenced by my experience in Sunday school growing up.

So, we decided that if we were going to raise a child, we would bring them up in the church. We also decided that if we wanted our children to be raised in the church, we were going to go with them. In 1996, I went to church for the first time in many, many years. I thought this was all about bringing a child up in the church. But God had even more in store for me.

I started reading my Bible, praying, worshipping, and meeting with others in small groups to study. I got involved in serving others and the God who seemed distant and far off when I was younger came near. I was convinced of my need for Him, and I was overwhelmed by His love for me. I decided that I wanted to make Jesus my life. I wanted to live *in relationship* with Christ. At this time in my life, God seemed so close and intimate. I couldn't get enough of worshipping, serving, and learning about God. My prayer life was so powerful and constant. I prayed throughout my day as I worked and as I drove my car. I fell asleep in conversation with the Lord and woke in the morning with a deep sense of God's presence. Once awake, we continued the conversation.

Throughout this time, I felt and responded to a call from God to pastoral ministry. I was really overwhelmed by the presence and power of God in this first year of my relationship with Christ. It was awesome and amazing. As I reflect on it and write about it now, it gives me "God bumps" – goose bumps brought on by the presence of God. I tell you this because it helps me understand the ease of playing church and not noticing.

I went from someone who was not a part of the church to someone serving the church in less than a year. I had figured out what I wanted to be when I grew up. I understood that God was calling me to be a pastor and I had begun to pursue that in the church. With the hunger and thirst I had for Jesus during this time, I began to pursue His calling for my life. My church at the time recognized and affirmed this calling and hired me as an associate pastor.

21

I went back to school to work on my educational requirements. I dove headlong into serving the church and living out God's calling on my life. For the next several years I was going to school, working in the church, and continued to develop and grow as a leader in the church. I finished my undergraduate and went to seminary. By then, Nicole and I had two more children. I took leadership of a building project at my home church when the senior pastor was moved at the start of the campaign. After that, I took a church of my own and led it as it grew numerically and spiritually in the two years that I served there before being called to lead another church in the denomination. At this time ministry was going well. My family life was good and it appeared that things were looking bright for the future.

It was the first week of January 2006 and I was at the monastery in Atchison, Kansas. The final class that I was taking for seminary was to immerse myself for a week in this community of Benedictine nuns. It was an incredible week of prayer, meditation, reading the psalms, and pursuing contemplative labor. I thoroughly enjoyed my week there even though it was not at the most opportune time for me in life and ministry. Perhaps it was at the perfect time, however, I did not see it that way at the time.

I had just moved to pastor the new church I mentioned earlier. It became a thriving, fruitful new start church that was growing and reaching new people. The church that I had just left had experienced significant growth spiritually and numerically. I had been going to seminary full time and pastoring full time. I was finally going to be finished with my formal education and be able to devote full time to pastoring and leading the church. I moved to my new church, preached my first sermon, and then left to go to the monastery. I left my wife at home with three children, a house full of unpacked boxes, in a place where she knew no one. I said I would be back in a week. It was not the best time to go away. Did I mention how amazing my wife is? She is amazing!

Ministry was going well. I had been studying, serving, and leading the church and outwardly everything was going well. I was busy and finally, I was going to be able to take seminary off my plate and focus full time on ministry in the church. As I sat in a barn that had been converted into an art studio, I was playing with a lump of clay and thinking about my relationship with God, it was like a window opened in my mind and I begin to have a conversation with God through that open window. Free-flowing open dialogue with God. At this moment, I was hit with one of the most powerful lessons about sin and about myself. I was taught how easy it is to play church and not even know it.

Good Things and God Things

Somewhere along the way, as I studied the Bible and theology, as I prepared and preached sermons, as I cared for the sick and tended to the saints, as I lead a church that was bearing fruit and growing... I had become separated from God. I was doing good things. I was not doing bad things. But, what I was doing had led me to a place where I was no longer connecting to God. Early on in my relationship with Christ, as I was falling in love with Jesus and hearing His call to ministry, that window in my mind remained open. I felt and experienced an open dialogue with God. This is what enabled me to discern and to follow where God was leading me. But, somewhere along the way in the midst of all the studying and church work, I had grown apart from God. Worse yet, I didn't even know it. I had not noticed that I had stopped the dialogue with God. I didn't recognize that the window had closed. I was so caught up doing good things that I stopped doing the *God things*. Good things can separate us from God. Church work can separate us from God. Good things can even become sin if we lose the connection from God's plan.

The other thing that I noticed is that people don't ask us whether we are doing the God things. In the church, for the most part, the people in my congregation were only concerned with what I was doing for them to help them in their relationship with God or what I was doing to serve them in their church. They were not asking me what I was doing to grow in my relationship with Christ. Nobody was asking about my prayer life or my spiritual growth. My district superintendents asked about worship attendance and giving. They didn't ask about my spiritual life.

We can get so caught up in *church* that we lose God and we end up *playing church*. The truth is that we can be good pastors, good church leaders, and good church folk. We can grow churches all while unknowingly playing church. What struck me at that time in my life, and still drives me today, is that I was not called to be a *good* pastor. I was not called to be a *great* pastor. I was called to be **God's** pastor. I could not and I would not play church. No matter how easy it is to slip into it, I refuse to play church.

Religion and Relationship

I know firsthand that it is easy for us to slip into playing church. We can get caught up in a kind of works righteousness that the Pharisees and the teachers of the law found themselves in without even noticing. We can exchange a relationship for religious practice. Religious practice is easy for us because it is easier than a relationship. We can schedule religious practices.

- Church every Sunday.
- Bible Study on Wednesday.
- Mission trip in the summer.

We can make them into lists and check off that we've done them. But unless they connect us to God and into the relationship that we are called to live with Him then they only help us to pretend we are something that we are not. They become props in our acting studio. They can become our own whitewashed tombs that are clean on the outside but destroy us on the inside. Empty rituals with no life-giving power. It is all about our relationship with God and our spiritual disciplines can and should connect us to Him. The end goal is to live in relationship with God and spiritual disciplines are a means to this end. As soon as we confuse the practice of religion with our relationship with God, we create an idol out of our practices. Those very practices, without the presence of God, will leave us empty.

A Faith that is Real

None of us go to church so that we can grow further from God. We all want a faith that is real. A faith that can move the mountains and slay the giants that we face in our lives. A faith that can calm our storms and sustain us through our life's dry lands and deep valleys. We want a faith that is empowered by the God who created us and promises to be with us always. We want a faith that connects us to the power of the resurrection and joins us in fellowship with Jesus in our sufferings and His. We want a faith that it is real. We want a real relationship with Jesus.

The good news is that it is possible. We *can* experience the power and presence of God in our ordinary, everyday lives. We can find calm and rest during our storms. We can see the mountains moved and giants defeated. Jesus promises us that He gives Himself to us to be in relationship with us, both now and forever. With that kind of relationship, we don't have to pretend that we are something that we are not. We don't have to be perfect and have it all together for Jesus to love us. Jesus loves us no matter what and He wants to *do life* with us. He invites us to live a new way of life with Him.

Chapter 4:
Getting Real

"But he said to me, "My grace is sufficient for you, for my power is made perfect in weakness." Therefore I will boast all the more gladly of my weaknesses, so that the power of Christ may rest upon me. For the sake of Christ, then, I am content with weaknesses, insults, hardships, persecutions, and calamities. For when I am weak, then I am strong" (2 Cor. 12:9-10).

"The greatest among you will be your servant. For those who exalt themselves will be humbled, and those who humble themselves will be exalted" (Matt. 23:11-12).

I want to refer again to the "first law of holes." If you have dug a hole for yourself and you want to get out of it, the first thing you must do is *stop digging*. We're using this analogy to help convey an understanding of the need to *stop playing church*. I would say that the first thing that we need to do if we are going to stop playing church is that we must *get real*. To stop playing church means that we will have to be real about who we are. We will have to take off the masks we use to portray the image we want. We will have to stop pretending.

We will have to be real about our weaknesses, struggles, and our dependence. If we want to get out of the hole of playing church, we must start by getting real. Be honest with ourselves. Honest with God. Honest with each other. We must be authentic, and our following of Jesus needs to be authentic as well. No more hiding. No more pretending. No more masks. No acting. Real. Step one: start getting real.

When I first came to church as an adult, I thought I was the only one there that did not have my life together. I was a young man, newly married, and about to have a child. I was afraid. I had, as they say, a "checkered past." I had been "far from God" to use church language. I had struggled with addiction and had no idea how to be married or raise children. I was struggling financially living paycheck to paycheck. I was trying to figure out what I wanted to be when I grew up even though I was already trying to grow up and be an adult. I was struggling in so many ways.

I'd thought I was the only one who struggled with life. It seemed to me that all the other people who were there had it all figured out. At least it appeared that way. They all looked happy. They all seemed to have their stuff together. I remember thinking if they really knew me, they would probably ask me to leave. If they knew the mess that I had been and the mess I still was, they would not want me messing up their church. So, I pretended that I was not a total mess. Inside I was empty, but I put on my Sunday best appearance, hoping to hide the emptiness while I went searching for something to fill it.

Thankfully, I got involved in a small group and got to know some people. I met some people who let me see behind their masks. They helped me see that God loved me just the way that I was, mess and all. I got to know my pastor and his wife, who allowed me to see that they were real and normal, just like me. As I got to know people, I realized that I was not alone in my struggles. Other people struggled too. What was hidden from me by the masks that we put on as we sat in rows, all came out of hiding when I sat in circles and got to know others. They began to share with me how Jesus had helped them in their struggles. How Jesus helps them in their weaknesses. I realized that I was not alone. I was not the only one who didn't have my stuff together. Through their vulnerability and willing-ness to share I came to understand my need for Jesus. I began to understand that the emptiness that I felt could be filled by Jesus. Jesus became real to me as we got real with each other. Well, they got real with me. I was still not willing to let them know the mess that I was. But I wanted Jesus and I knew I needed Him. I asked Him to come to fill my emptiness, forgive me, and to be my life.

The small group was just a short-term study that lasted for six weeks. During that time I was reading my Bible every day, praying, worshipping, and spending time each week with the small group. At the end of our six weeks, I was invited to share what the small group meant to me during a Sunday service. Truth be told, I hadn't said too much during those six weeks in the small group. I did a lot of listening, reading, praying, and seeking Jesus. I am sure that many people in the group were surprised when I said I would share something because I had not shared much in the group. I am really an introvert. That Sunday, I shared how God had become real to me during this time and how I had asked Jesus to come into my life. But I still had my mask on.

As I shared in the previous chapter, during this time my relationship with Jesus was powerful and I really felt connected to God. I was praying seemingly continuously. I was seeing God working in me and in my life. I was seeking to know Jesus with all that I had.

One day, I was driving home from work, and I had a thought go through my mind. The thought was, "You are my stories." I am sure that I moved on to other thoughts, but I returned to that thought because it struck me. My thought was not "I am His stories," it was "You are My stories." After that, I thought, "Could God be talking to me?" My next thought was, "Am I Crazy?"

I drove to my pastor's house; he was not home so I asked his wife to tell me that I was not crazy. She did but she said I should probably talk to the pastor. When he and I spoke, he told me it sounded like I needed to tell people my story. I remember telling him, *I don't think people want to hear my story.* If they really knew me, they would turn me away. If they knew that I had struggled with drug addiction and battled with depression. If they knew that I had gotten to such a low and empty place that I didn't love anyone, not even myself, and that I'd tried to take my own life, they would reject me. They would not want me messing up their church. He asked me to pray about sharing my story with the men's group the following week. I did, and it was at this point that I began to see the power of my own vulnerability.

I was not rejected, in fact, people showed me grace and love. I was not turned away, but instead, people began to open up to me about having similar struggles and difficulties. I also discovered that Jesus can use our messes for His glory and to relate to others. We don't have to have it all figured out. We don't have to have our stuff together for Jesus to do what Jesus promises He will do. We don't have to be someone else to be used by Jesus and we don't have to pretend that we are better than we really are. We just need to be real.

What would happen if we really took seriously the teachings of Jesus and took off our masks, stopped hiding, quit pretending, stopped playing a part, and just got real? What if we became real about the people that we were and are now? Real about our love. Real about our relationship with God. I know that I have learned over the past twenty-plus years since making Jesus my life and serving Him in pastoral ministry, that we tap into the power of God and grow in our relationship with Jesus and others as we get real about who we are. We experience Christ's strength In our weaknesses. We are lifted up when we humble ourselves and are honest about our need for Jesus.

One of the masks that we wear in our culture is the *mask of independence*. We try to convince ourselves that we can do it ourselves. We don't need anyone. Self-sufficient. Self-reliant. However, we are all weak and in need of each other. I think that the great myth of our culture (and we do everything we can to perpetuate it) is that we are not weak, fragile, broken people in need of others – and in need of God. We were created by God to be in community, to be dependent on one another. Yet, we shake our bony fists at God and say *we can do it on our own*. We put on Superman capes and Wonder Woman bracelets and we pretend that we are independent and even bullet-proof.

When we try to do it all on our own, it just makes us more fragile and more broken. Then we must try even harder to hide our weaknesses and not let others see us as we truly are. Getting real requires us to be honest about our dependence on God for everything. Getting real requires us to be honest about our need for each other. We are not meant to be alone. We need each other. It is amazing when we understand just how weak we really are and that we need Jesus and each other. In these moments we experience the strength and power of God. His power is made perfect in our weakness.

When we are ready to stop playing church then it is time to get real about who we are. Stop hiding and take off our masks. We need to find people with whom we can be vulnerable.

This is probably not going to happen, in fact, I suggest it probably shouldn't happen in a large setting. It happens in small groups. It happens with friends who are committed to growing together in relationship with Christ. If we are going to stop playing church, we must start being honest about our need for God and our need for each other.

Getting real also requires us to take the teachings of Jesus seriously. It requires us to get real about our love for God and our love for others. It requires us to get real about following Jesus in the ordinary, everyday moments of our lives. It requires us to get real about loving our neighbors as Christ loves us. It requires authentic discipleship that is a lived faith, not a checklist, a to-do list, or a program that we can hide behind or exchange for a relationship with Jesus.

It requires authentic discipleship that is a way of life in and through Christ, one that connects us to God and others and develops us into the people that we are called to be. Having an authentic discipleship leads to the transformation of who we are so that we become like Jesus. A way of life that allows Christ to transform us to be more and more like Him. An authentic discipleship is about being in relationship with Jesus and not focusing solely on *doing*.

But first, we have to stop digging and we have to start getting real. Real about the people that we are. Real about our love. Real about our relationship with God.

Part II:
Authentic Discipleship and Spiritual Disciplines

Chapter 5:
Being and Doing

Are you tired? Worn out? Burned out on religion? Come to me. Get away with me and you'll recover your life. I'll show you how to take a real rest. Walk with me and work with me— watch how I do it. Learn the unforced rhythms of grace. I won't lay anything heavy or ill-fitting on you. Keep company with me and you'll learn to live freely and lightly.

Matthew 11:28-30 (MSG)

In the first part of this book, I have tried to lay out what playing church is and why it is so important that we stop. In part two, I want to suggest a new way of understanding the church and discipleship that has been helpful for me. Over the past twenty years, as I have been trying to live and become a much more authentic expression of my faith. I have worked on being real about who I am, real about my love for God and my love for my neighbor. I have discovered that for me to make the shift from playing church to not playing church – it required me to shift my paradigm of what church and discipleship are. I have also found this shift in my thinking helpful for me as a church leader as I seek to help facilitate people in living out their relationship with Jesus.

For centuries when people have talked about the church and discipleship, their focus has been on *doing*. What does the church do? What do disciples do? We identify the things that we need to do as the church and then we organize committees, programs, activities and hire staff so that we are doing what churches do. We develop discipleship plans, programs, resources all to help disciples do what they are supposed to do. The focus is always on doing. Well, not always on doing. Sometimes we talk about what not to do. "Churches don't do that." "That is not discipleship." But this is still focused on *doing*.

Here's the thing, when our paradigm is all about doing, it becomes too easy to replace or substitute our relationship with Jesus with *the things we are busily doing*. "I go to church so I must be a Christian," or "I read my Bible, I pray, I worship... so I am following Jesus." People give of their time or money and say, "I am serving and doing mission trips, so I am following Jesus." While these are all good things to do, they can just be masks or whitewashed tombs. They can give the appearance of following Jesus, but they can also just be activities that people do without ever knowing Jesus.

The problem isn't the doing. We will always be doing things. We are doers. The problem is a thinking and understanding that tries to define a relationship by something other than that relationship. An understanding of church and discipleship that focuses on what we do creates the opportunity to slip off the slippery slope of playing church. If we want to be authentic and real about our relationship with Christ if we want to stop playing church, we need to shift the focus off of what we do and put the focus on our relationship with Jesus.

I have found the biblical understanding of the Sabbath helpful in shifting my thinking on the church and discipleship. You see, Sabbath is not about doing and is all about being in relationship with God. While many of the church people of Jesus's day thought that Sabbath was about doing. Actually, on the Sabbath, they were focused on *not doing*. They didn't do anything on the Sabbath. So, when Jesus came along and healed people on the Sabbath and His disciples picked some grain to eat, you can imagine the people whose paradigm was on *doing* and *not doing*, got pretty upset that Jesus and his followers would be doing anything on the Sabbath. One of the many things that Jesus tries to teach them and to teach us is that they are focused on the wrong thing. Sabbath is God's gift to God's people to be in relationship with Him. To trust. To rest. Be restored and renewed by being in relationship with God. It is not about what we do. It is about who we are being. Are we being in relationship with God or are we just not doing anything on the Sabbath? Are we making Jesus Lord of the Sabbath or are we just focused on not doing anything? Jesus invites them and us to shift the paradigm about Sabbath from *doing* to *being*.

What if this is what we need to do with our understanding of the church and discipleship? What if we began from a place of being in relationship with Christ and lived in relationship with Christ rather than just *doing*? What if our understanding of church was living in relationship with Jesus and relationship with one another? What if church is understood from a place of who we are being and what we are becoming rather than what we are doing? What if we saw discipleship in the same way? Not that there are not things that we do but that is not the focus.

After all, isn't *being* what Jesus invited us to do in Matthew 11? *"Are you tired? Worn out? Burned out on religion? Come to me. Get away with me and you'll recover your life. I'll show you how to take a real rest. Walk with me and work with me— watch how I do it. Learn the unforced rhythms of grace. I won't lay anything heavy or ill-fitting on you. Keep company with me and you'll learn to live freely and lightly."* He invites us to be in relationship with Him. To be. To rest in Him as Lord of our lives. Keep company with Him. Focus on being first.

I want to suggest that this is exactly the shift that is necessary for us to authentically live-in relationship with Jesus and steer away from the slippery slope of playing church. I believe that a shift of thinking that focuses on Jesus being Lord of our lives and being in relationship with Jesus over what we are doing is necessary if we want to get real about not playing church. This shift does not mean we don't do things. It means that our focus and priority is on our being over our doing. Being comes first and our doing flows from our being.

What I am suggesting is not just a change in our language. I am suggesting a shift in church culture and how we think about being the church. In the next few chapters, I will share with you how I have shifted the way that I think what the church is with this new paradigm and how I am understanding what I call authentic discipleship. I will try to get practical because I know we all have the tendency to fall into the mind of doers. We are good with the being paradigm, but we would like to know what we do while we are being. I want to say something to church leaders at this point, but it is really for everyone to hear. This shift from doing to being is much more organic than it is organized. It is not as easily programmed, planned, and duplicated. It is about being not about doing. The challenge for church leaders and those helping people to live in relationship with Christ is that we need to try to organize the organic. We need to help people to see how they can arrange their being in such a way that it connects them to God and others and helps them grow in relationship with Christ. Also, this does not mean that we throw out all the stuff that we have been doing like worship, ministry, missions, discipleship, evangelism it means that we have the tasks of reimagining them within the paradigm of being and doing. I find it helpful with my staff and with the people who plan and organize ministry to have them think about creating space and opportunity for people to connect to God and others and live out their relationship with Jesus. We want to nurture people in growing in their relationship with God and others by creating opportunities for them to do life together in Christ. We do not want to create to-do list or boxes to fill. We do not want to limit the organic nature of our relationship with Christ by organizing it too stringently. We need to maintain the organic nature while helping people organize their understanding of being and doing church and following Jesus.

One last thing on paradigm shifts before we move on. A shift in our way of thinking is not as easy as just changing some words.

It is important to understand that changing a culture is not easy and it does not happen overnight. I did not change how I think overnight, I certainly shouldn't expect an organized religious institution to change overnight. The church has understood what the church does for centuries and for many people they are simply fine with the way things are. When we start to talk about changing our way of thinking and being the church, we will have resistance. Much of it will be because we just have never thought about it this way and even when we try to reimagine church, we are still trapped in the understanding of the things that we have always been doing. So, don't be discouraged if at first people think you are crazy and you don't know what you are talking about. Live it. Get real about your relationship with Jesus. Don't hide. Don't pretend. Refuse to play church and begin to live the new way of life that Christ calls you to. Get real about your love for God and your love for your neighbor. Set your thoughts and your focus on being in relationship with God and living it out every day. Make being a priority over doing.

Chapter 6:
Doing Life Together

They devoted themselves to the apostles' teaching and to fellowship, to the breaking of bread and to prayer. Everyone was filled with awe at the many wonders and signs performed by the apostles. All the believers were together and had everything in common. They sold property and possessions to give to anyone who had need. Every day they continued to meet together in the temple courts. They broke bread in their homes and ate together with glad and sincere hearts, praising God and enjoying the favor of all the people. And the Lord added to their number daily those who were being saved.

Acts 2:42-47

If we are going to begin with *being* over doing and if *being* is the priority over doing, how should we talk about what the church is? What is the church in the context of being in relationship with Christ and others? As important as getting real is to not playing church, there is also an equally important matter to consider. If we want to stop playing church, we must be clear about what church is. I think it is helpful to develop an understanding of church that is biblical and not bound by things that we can hide behind or replace for a relationship with Jesus. We need an understanding of church that focuses on being first and then doing. An understanding of church where what the church does flows form who the church is being in relationship with Jesus. After all, we don't want to make church a replacement for our relationship with Jesus. People have done that for years and it is killing them. We have already established that it is easy to mistake church attendance and churchy things for our relationship with Jesus. Maybe it is because we have too narrow of an understanding of what church is?

I think for the most part we all have learned that the church is not a building. Even though we call our buildings churches. We know that church is more than that, yet we still tend to think about going to church more than we think about being the church. Many have broadened their understanding of church to be the people. No building necessary. We draw on the biblical imagery of the "Body of Christ" and being "living stones". While I think these images clarify our need for one another and our dependance upon each other to grow in relationship with Jesus. I still feel that it may not be broad enough to fully understand what church is.

I find it helpful, to gain a broader understanding of church, to look at the community of people who were the first ones trying to live in and live out their relationship with Jesus. The ones who were following Jesus after the resurrection and before anything had been organized called "Christianity" or anything had been called "church". Acts chapter 2 is where we get the first writing about the early church. It is right after Pentecost. Pentecost is considered the birth of the "church". Again, it is important to note that in the first century it was not being called this. The only name given to this group of followers in the book of Acts is "the way."[5] They were people of "the way." They were living a certain way. As we look to them, we see that after the Holy Spirit fell upon all of them, at Pentecost, they started to live out and live in relationship with Christ who had filled them with the Holy Spirit. We read that they got real about living out their relationship with Jesus. The took seriously the teaching of Jesus and applied them to their everyday living.

What we don't read is that they got together once a week, or that they got together to do mission projects or for bible studies. What we see is that they began to do life together. They shared their lives with each other, and they depended on each other. They were connecting to God and connecting to one another. They were helping each other grow in relationship with Christ by doing life together. They were taking seriously their relationship with God and their relationships with each other. They were devoted to God and deeply committed to each other. They were learning from the Apostles teachings and they were putting those teachings into practice in their everyday ordinary lives as they lived in community with each other. They cared for, supported, nurtured, and celebrated one another as they lived in relationship with Christ and one each other. We read that *"Every day they continued to meet together in the temple courts. They broke bread in their homes*

---

[5] Acts 9:2; 19:9, 23; 22:4; 24:14, 22

and ate together with glad and sincere hearts, praising God and enjoying the favor of all the people."[6] They were doing life together because that is what being empowered by the Holy Spirit and being devoted to their relationship with Christ was compelling them to do. Their being real about their love for God and their love for their neighbor compelled them so much that *"All the believers were together and had everything in common. They sold property and possessions to give to anyone who had need."[7]*

For these early followers it appears that church was a 24/7 thing. It seems as if church was anything and everything that they were doing. It was who they were, and it was how they were living their lives. Church was a way of life. For these people of the way it appears that there is no line drawn between what is spiritual and what is secular. They lived out their relationship with God as they lived their lives. They did life with Jesus as they worked, as they played, as they gathered for dinner parties and as they gathered for communion. They lived out their relationship with God in the temple courts and in their homes. This way of life that they were living was tapping into the power of God and they were seeing miracles happening all around them. As they lived in and out their relationship with Christ, being real about who they were and being real about their relationship with God, more and more people were drawn to do life with Jesus and do life with them. Clearly, these people of the way were living a completely different way than the world around them was living. They understood

---

[6] Acts 2:46

[7] Acts 2:44-45

church as a way of life. It was not a confined to a building, an activity, a certain group of people (the group kept growing every day), or a place. Church is a way of life that connects us to God and others. That takes seriously being in relationship with Christ and living it out every moment of every day. Church is a way of life.

What would happen if we began to understand church as a way of life? What if we began to see that living out our relationship, and living in relationship with Jesus, takes place all the time? What if we began to understand that there is no separation between the spiritual and the secular? What if we began to see that Jesus is inviting us to live a new way of life with Him? What if we began to see that church is a 24/7 way of doing life together like they lived following Pentecost in the first century? What kind of wonders and signs do you think we might see?

This understanding of church is broad enough for us to keep the focus on being in relationship with God and opens our understanding to see that anything that we do can connect us to God and others and help us to grow in relationship with Christ. It is important to note that it is not just any way of life. It is a particular way of life. The early church lived differently than the world around them. Church was a 24/7 way of living and doing life with one another that flowed out of their being in relationship with Christ. This way of life flowed from and was empowered by the Spirit that lived in each of them. It is a particular way of life. Church is a way of life that flows from the power of the Holy Spirit within us and flows from our being in relationship with God. It is also a way of life that continues to connect us to God and others and continues to empower us with the Holy Spirit. It is a way of live that continues to nurture, care for, support, and celebrate our being in relationship with Christ and one another. The primary focus is on being and becoming. The doing comes from the being. It comes from doing life with Jesus and one another. It is organic, not highly organized, and it is real life.

Chapter 7:
Church as a Way of Life

Jesus, undeterred, went right ahead and gave his charge: "God authorized and commanded me to commission you: Go out and train everyone you meet, far and near, in this way of life, marking them by baptism in the threefold name: Father, Son, and Holy Spirit. Then instruct them in the practice of all I have commanded you. I'll be with you as you do this, day after day after day, right up to the end of the age."

Matthew 28:18-20 (The Message)

I f we understand church as a particular way of life and that church is 24/7 living in and living out our relationship with Christ, then how do we understand the mission of the church? Most churches understand that the mission of the church is given by Jesus in Matthew 28:18-20 in what is often referred to as the "Great Commission." Jesus says, "*Therefore go and make disciples of all nations, baptizing them in the name of the Father and of the Son and of the Holy Spirit.*"[8]

---

[8] Matthew 28:19, New International Version

Discipleship is a word that is not used in many contexts. The church is really the only place that we use the word. We often think of the twelve men who followed Jesus as disciples, but we don't often think of ourselves that way. Churches understand that their mission is to make disciples. But what does that mean? Too often, we create discipleship programs, committees, plans, and studies but these can all become facades that we can hide being and even programs to fool us into thinking that we are living in relationship with Jesus. They can become scholarly endeavors that help us to know about Jesus but are not really focused on *being in relationship with Jesus*.

I am not at all suggesting that the mission of the church is somehow different because we shift our understanding of what we mean by *the church*. I still believe that the mission of the church is to help others become disciples. So, how are we to understand disciple-making in a context where it can be easy to substitute what we are doing for our relationship with Christ?

How can we imagine discipleship in the context of a way of life together and be in relationship with Jesus? Well, it is helpful to find another word. When we read *The Message*, a modern biblical translation that uses language that we are familiar with, it does not use the word *disciple* in Jesus's "Great Commission." Instead, Peterson, the translator, interprets it as *"Go out and train everyone you meet, far and near, in this way of life."*[9] Making disciples in contemporary language is training people in this way of life. This might be useful. What if we think about

---

[9] Matthew 28:19, The Message

discipleship within the context of being the church? What if we look at discipleship as part of this way of life called church?

If we begin to understand that church is a way of life, then discipleship is training in this way of life. It is training people to do life together *in relationship with Jesus*. It is creating space and opportunity to connect to God and others. It is training to be in relationship with Jesus. It is inviting and equipping people to live a new way of life that is *church*. Inviting people to do life together, being real about who they are, real about their relationship with Jesus, and real about their love for God and others. You are inviting people to a 24/7 life together that is empowered by the Holy Spirit and is focused on being in relationship with God. It is a life where all that we do flows from the empowerment of the Holy Spirit and living in and living out our relationship with Jesus.

Discipleship then, is helping people to be the church and not play church. Discipleship is helping people get real about who they are. Discipleship is helping people get real about being in relationship with Jesus and doing life with Him. Discipleship is about helping people live in love with Jesus and live out the love of Jesus in real, tangible ways. Discipleship is about helping people make Jesus their life, not just an accessory that they attach to their lives. It is about getting real about living the new way of life that Jesus invites us to live *in community* with one another, being empowered by the Holy Spirit. It is about helping one another grow in relationship with Jesus.

This idea of discipleship suggests that we need to train people that church is a way of life. We need to help people be devoted to their relationship with God and *live in relationship with Him*. It suggests that we need to help people become deeply committed to one another and to live out their love for God in relationship with others. Church is not a solo endeavor. We are not church by ourselves; it is a way of life lived in community with other people. We need to help people have a broader understanding of what Jesus is calling them for. We need to help people recognize the presence of Christ in their lives and help them tap into the power of God in the ordinary everyday moments of life. This idea of discipleship means we need to help people tear down the walls that we build to separate our spiritual lives from the rest of our lives.

An understanding of authentic discipleship as training in church as a way of life means that we must be able to identify what this way of life is. Remember, the focus is on *being*, so we have to be able to identify not what we do, but what we are and what we are becoming. We need to identify what character traits are necessary for us to *be the church* and live this Christ-centered way of life.

What is it about our way of life and who we are being that enables us to connect to God and grow in our relationship with Christ 24/7 in all that we do, living our lives? Remember, the church in Acts lived a particular way of life that was different from the way other people lived. If we are going to train people in this new way of life, we have to be able to identify some markers, some characteristics, and some habits that are part of the fiber of being a church. What characteristics are developed in our lives as we live in relationship with Christ?

What characteristics are developed as we become more like Christ as we do life together?

This is the piece of the organic nature that is necessary for church leaders and others to organize. Remembe,r we are not looking for a to-do list, we want to identify the personal characteristics and outcomes that mark this way of life. When we can identify these then we can begin to train people in this new way of life. And we can know that this way of life is enabling us to be real about our relationship with God and grow in relationship with Him. Then we can identify what the particular way of life is that we are called to live and live out the mission that Jesus gives us to train everyone in this way of life.

I want to start with *outcome*. If we are being disciples, following Jesus, and growing in relationship with Christ, then our character, the people we are, will be more like Jesus. Paul says that in 2 Corinthians 3:17-18, *"Now the Lord is the Spirit, and where the Spirit of the Lord is, there is freedom. And we all, who with unveiled faces contemplate the Lord's glory, are being transformed into his image with ever-increasing glory, which comes from the Lord, who is the Spirit."* As we live this way of life we should become more like Jesus. Paul writes in Galatians about the characteristics that bear fruit in our lives as we are transformed to be more like Jesus. He writes, "But the fruit of the Spirit is love, joy, peace, forbearance, kindness, goodness, faithfulness, gentleness and self-control."[10] A way of life that is empowered by the Holy Spirit – one that is lived

---

[10] Galatians 5:22-23a, New International Version

24/7 in relationship with Jesus and is growing will be marked by these characteristics.

We can't measure our spiritual growth by how many times we read our Bible cover to cover or if we read it at all. We can't measure our spiritual growth by worship or Sunday School attendance or the number of Bible studies we take part in. According to Paul, if we are living in relationship with Christ and growing in that relationship, we will be more and more loving, joyful, peaceful, patient, kind, good, faithful, gentle, and self-controlled. Jesus said, "I am the vine; you are the branches. If you remain in me and I in you, you will bear much fruit; apart from me you can do nothing. (John 15:5)." We can identify that disciples, followers of Jesus, people living this way of life called the church will develop and bear these fruits of the Spirit in their lives. If the way of life we are living is not developing these characteristics in us then we are not living a way of life that is connecting us to God. We are not living in relationship with Jesus. If our life together is not helping us to love God more and love our neighbor more than it is not church. Period. Your life and my life should be characterized by these fruits of the Spirit and they should be ever-growing if we are being real about our relationship with Jesus.

These characteristics develop over time and they help us to live in and live out our relationship with Christ. They certainly give us evidence that what we are doing is connecting us to God and growing us in relationship with Jesus. They can help us to see if we are fulfilling the mission of the church as we see people connecting to God and becoming more and more like Jesus. These are fruits of the Spirit are not fruits of you and me. Apart from Jesus, we can't bear these fruits. So, they help us to see that God is working in our lives. I have also found it helpful to identify some characteristics of church as a way of life that are not just an outcome or produced in us but help give structure to the way of life that we are called to live while maintaining the organic nature of our relationship with Jesus. These characteristics – intentionality, humility, vulnerability, authenticity, and integrity are vital characteristics for doing life together.

If we are going to be the church and do life together then we must be intentional about it. We must live humbly, not taking ourselves too seriously or thinking we are better than we are. We must take off our masks and stop pretending. We must be real and authentic about who we are and our need for God and one another. Finally, we must be people who do what we say we will do.

When we look at the first followers of Jesus, we see that these characteristics mark their lives together. There, community was Christ-centered and Spirit-empowered because they were intentional about their relationship with Jesus and their commitment to one another. They were intentional about loving God and loving one another. They were open about their needs and their need for each another, and they were real about who they were and whose they were. The lived in and lived out their relationship with Jesus in real and tangible ways 24/7 no matter where they were because they were devoted to God and committed to one another. They were intentional, humble, vulnerable, authentic, and had integrity.

We are empowered by the same Spirit even today. Jesus invites us to stop playing church and get real about who we are. To get real about our love of God and get real about living in relationship with Him. He invites us to a new way of life that is focused on being overdoing and lived every moment of every day. He has a place for you and me in this way of life called the church.

Chapter 8:
Authentic Discipleship and Real Spiritual Habits

*They devoted themselves to the apostles'
teaching and to fellowship, to the breaking of
bread and to prayer. Everyone was filled with
awe at the many wonders and signs performed
by the apostles. All the believers were together
and had everything in common. They sold
property and possessions to give to anyone who
had need. Every day they continued to meet
together in the temple courts. They broke bread
in their homes and ate together with glad and
sincere hearts, praising God and enjoying the
favor of all the people. And the Lord added to
their number daily those who were being saved.*

Acts 2:42-47

We won't stop playing church just because we have read a book about it or because we have written one. If we really want to have something happen, we must be intentional about it. God loves us and desires a relationship with us, but he also loves us enough that he doesn't force that relationship on us. If we want to live in relationship with Jesus, we must be intentional about doing it in our lives. We must be intentional about doing the things that connect us to God. It really doesn't just happen. We don't grow in relationship with God merely by chance. It takes deliberate action. If we are going to stop playing church, we have to get intentional about taking off our makes and coming out of hiding. We have to be intentional about being vulnerable about our struggles, our difficulties, and even our struggles with connecting to God.

We have to be vulnerable in our friendships and relationships and admit our need for God and each other. Nothing will happen just by chance. If we are going to live church as a way of life, we will have to be intentional about doing life together and making Christ a part of everything we do. We will have to be intentional about recognizing that Christ is with us in our homes, our workplaces, at the grocery store, the coffee shop, the restaurant, and even the bar. We must be intentional about recognizing Jesus is present in the communion meal and he is present with us at all other meals. We will have to be intentional about making Christ the center of everything that we do and all our relationships. Doing life together in Christ takes intentionally humbling ourselves and being intentional about doing what we say we will do.

Authentic discipleship is a way of doing life together that is marked by the characteristics of intentionality, humility, authenticity, vulnerability, and integrity. It is not a program, a plan, or to-do list. It is a way of living that connects us to God and others in the ordinary everyday moments of life and enables us to grow in relationship with Christ and develops a deepening love of God and love of our neighbors.

As we look at the church in Acts, we can see that they are doing certain things that flow out of who they are and whose they are. We can see that their relationship and devotion to God lead to certain habits in their lives. Those established habits help them to continue to tap into the power of the Holy Spirit and to live in and live out their relationship with God. These practices are a part of their everyday lives and are vital to their doing life together in and through Christ. We are told that they are devoted to applying the teachings of the Apostles to their lives, they are devoted to being together, they are devoted to worship and prayer. They served each other and they shared their faith with others. As they did life together these habits helped shape them and shape their lives together. These habits helped them connect to God in their ordinary, everyday lives.

Authentic discipleship needs to develop real spiritual habits in our lives. As we do live together, as the church, we need to be connecting to God and tapping into the power that only God can provide. We need real spiritual habits that flow out of our *being in relationship with Christ* and help us develop that relationship. But what we can't do is allow these habits to replace our relationship with God. Authentic discipleship recognizes that these are important habits that help us to connect and grow in relationship with God, but they cannot and will not serve as a substitute for living in relationship with Christ. They are a part of the way of life that God calls us to. That being said, as we do life together, we need to be doing certain spiritual disciplines because they are activities that enable us to encounter God and then continue to grow in relationship with Christ. These are the activities that we see continually happening in the first-century church and they are activities that we can be intentional about doing authentically in our lives as we do life together

As church leaders and those who are trying to organize the organic nature of church as a way of life and living in relationship with Jesus, we need to create space and opportunity for people to participate and develop these habits in their lives. The habits that I am referring to are prayer, worship, biblical teaching, Christian interaction or fellowship, service, and faith sharing. If we are to help people to live the way of life that we are called to as the church, these are tools to help us reach that goal. As church leaders, it is our job to help people to see these as habits that must be developed because they help us grow in and live out our relationship with Christ, but they are no substitute for living in relationship with God. We also need to model, teach, and incorporate these habits in all that we do.

Our tendency at this point, and even as I write this, I fight my own inclinations to turn this into a program. To say okay, authentic discipleship is _____. And authentic discipleship looks like _____.

In the appendix, I share with you a few things that we use to talk about and frame our doing living together at North Star. However, it is not something that can just be duplicated and then we are all doing authentic discipleship. No, authentic discipleship is not neat and tidy. It is messy because it is real life. Authentic discipleship flows from a community of people being real about who they are, who God is, and real about living in relationship with Christ. It flows from people being in relationship with Christ and each other. It flows from a community of people being intentional, humble, authentic, vulnerable, and having integrity. Authentic discipleship is life lived in an authentic, biblically functioning, Christ-centered, and Spirit-empowered community. That last sentence sounded really *churchy* I know, but it is also true.

As church leaders, our focus should be on helping our communities be Christ-centered and Spirit-empowered. We need to help our people understand and apply biblical teaching to their lives. We need to help people to see their lives and all that they do together as the training up in this new way of life that is the church. We need to help them develop the important characteristics that mark this new way of life. More importantly, we need to help them to develop real spiritual habits that connect them to God and enable God to do what only God can do— make us more and more like Jesus.

If we want to help people to stop playing church then we must be communities that refuse to play church. We need to be communities where it ok not to be ok. We need to be communities that are not perfect or have it all figured out. We need to be communities of people who understand our dependence and fight our independence. We need communities that are vulnerable and humble. We need to be serious about our love for God and our love for one another. We need to be devoted to Christ and committed to doing life together. We must stop playing church and get real about *being* the church.

This is my authentic *discipleship plan.*

Appendix

THE NORTH STAR WAY

Church is a way of doing life together marked by the characteristics of Intentionality, Humility, Vulnerability, Authenticity, **and** *Integrity. It is a way of living that Gathers, Prays,* **and** *Loves and develops the habits of:*

- SPIRIT-EMPOWERED **PRAYER**
- LIFE-CHANGING **WORSHIP**
- LIFE APPLICATION **OF THE BIBLE**
- RISK-TAKING **MISSIONS AND SERVICE**
- CHRIST-INFUSED **FRIENDSHIPS**
- COURAGEOUS & CONTAGIOUS **FAITH SHARING**

#doinglifetogether

DOING LIFE TOGETHER @NORTH STAR CHURCH

GATHER   PRAY   LOVE

North Star Strategic Focus

"Doing Life Together"

North Star will focus on being a community gathering place where people do life together. We will create space and opportunity for people to develop Christ-infused friendships that are authentic and intentional about connecting to God and each other, helping each other grow in relationship with Christ, and caring and supporting one another through life's ups and downs.

5 Areas of Emphasis

> **Connect** – connect people to God and others.
> **Nurture** – grow in relationship with God and others.
> **Care** – carry one another's burdens, help each other, serve one another.
> **Support** – laugh, cry, encourage, and inspire one another.
> **Celebrate** – enjoy life and one another, worship as a life-style, have fun.

Acknowledgements

There are so many people who have had an impact on me throughout my life and have brought me to the writing of this book. Many people had more faith and confidence in me than I did at times. I want to begin by thanking my parents for all the love and support they gave me throughout my life. I was a kid who was blessed to be part of a large, blended family, growing up. My parents, Jacque VanBlarcum and Dave Franklin were my first and often loudest cheerleaders. To my stepparents, Maryle Franklin and Dave VanBlarcum, thank you for all of your love, caring, and support. To all my siblings, you have each had a part in making me into who I am. I love you all.

As I think about writing a book about being the church and church leadership, I have so many churches, pastors, mentors, and colleagues that I stand on the shoulders of today. I have to thank Pastor Jon Spalding and the congregation of Pleasant Hill United Methodist Church in Pleasant Hill, Missouri for being the pastor and the church that introduced me to Jesus. You not only helped me see Jesus as real, but you were the first to recognize the call that God had on my life to pastoral ministry.

This book has been made possible because of the congregations that I have been able to do life with as I have grown and developed as a leader. Thank you to Smith Chapel, Prairie Chapel, and Dockery Chapel. Thank you to the congregation of North Star United Methodist Church for being the playground and classroom for authentic discipleship. Thank you to the staff, leadership, and church family for your intentionality, humility, authenticity, vulnerability, and integrity as we gather, pray and love together.

I am grateful for my Friday morning coffee friends, Shawn and Buck, who have been with me from the beginning of this ministry journey and will forever challenge and inspire me in this way of life.

Several years ago, I spoke out loud to someone other than Nicole that I felt God was calling me to write a book. It was a small group that I was a part of at the time and we were sharing with each other about God-sized dreams. This group helped to pray this into existence. I want to thank my friends, Carol and Allan Seidel, for never giving up on this dream and continuing to encourage and prod me to write the book. Thanks for providing me a place to finish it up.

I am grateful to my wife Nicole and my children, Tucker, Tanner, Delaney, and Darbey. Ministry is a calling that involves and impacts the entire family. Words can't describe how much I appreciate the sacrifices you have all made for me to pursue this calling. You guys are my greatest work.

Ultimately, I thank God, because He is the giver of all these good and perfect gifts – which I have only named a few. If there is any good to come out of this work, it is for His glory and it is because of Him, not me.